'But I, while
vineyards ring
with the cicadas'
scream, Retrace
your steps, alone,
beneath the
burning sun.'

D0453397

PUBLIUS VERGILIUS MARO
Born 70 BCE, Mantua, Italy
Died 19 BCE, Brindisi, Italy

This selection is taken from Guy Lee's translation of *The Eclogues*,
first published in 1980, and Kimberly Johnson's translation of
The Georgics, first published in 2009.

VIRGIL IN PENGUIN CLASSICS
The Aeneid
The Eclogues
The Georgics

VIRGIL

O Cruel Alexis

Translated by
Guy Lee and Kimberly Johnson

PENGUIN BOOKS

PENGUIN CLASSICS

Published by the Penguin Group
Penguin Books Ltd, 80 Strand, London WC2R ORL, England
Penguin Group (USA) Inc., 375 Hudson Street, New York, New York 10014, USA
Penguin Group (Canada), 90 Eglinton Avenue East, Suite 700, Toronto, Ontario,
Canada M4P 2Y3 (a division of Pearson Penguin Canada Inc.)
Penguin Ireland, 25 St Stephen's Green, Dublin 2, Ireland
(a division of Penguin Books Ltd)
Penguin Group (Australia), 707 Collins Street, Melbourne, Victoria 3008, Australia
(a division of Pearson Australia Group Pty Ltd)
Penguin Books India Pvt Ltd, 11 Community Centre, Panchsheel Park,
New Delhi – 110 017, India
Penguin Group (NZ), 67 Apollo Drive, Rosedale, Auckland 0632, New Zealand
(a division of Pearson New Zealand Ltd)
Penguin Books (South Africa) (Pty) Ltd, Block D, Rosebank Office Park,
181 Jan Smuts Avenue, Parktown North, Gauteng 2193, South Africa

Penguin Books Ltd, Registered Offices: 80 Strand, London WC2R ORL, England

www.penguin.com

This selection published in Penguin Classics 2015
001

Translation copyright © Guy Lee, 1980, 1984
Translation copyright © Kimberly Johnson, 2009

All rights reserved
Without limiting the rights under copyright
reserved above, no part of this publication may be
reproduced, stored in or introduced into a retrieval system,
or transmitted, in any form or by any means (electronic, mechanical,
photocopying, recording or otherwise), without the prior
written permission of both the copyright owner and
the above publisher of this book

Set in 9/12.4 pt Baskerville 10 Pro
Typeset by Jouve (UK), Milton Keynes
Printed in Great Britain by Clays Ltd, St Ives plc

A CIP catalogue record for this book is available from the British Library

ISBN: 978–0–141–39873–0

www.greenpenguin.co.uk

MIX
Paper from
responsible sources
FSC
www.fsc.org
FSC™ C018179

Penguin Books is committed to a sustainable
future for our business, our readers and our planet.
This book is made from Forest Stewardship
Council™ certified paper.

Contents

Eclogue I

MELIBOEUS   TITYRUS

M. Tityrus, lying back beneath wide beechen cover,
     You meditate the woodland Muse on slender oat;
     We leave the boundaries and sweet ploughlands of
         home.
     We flee our homeland; you, Tityrus, cool in shade,
     Are teaching woods to echo *Lovely Amaryllis*.
T. Oh, Melibóeus, a god has made this leisure ours.
     Yes, he will always be a god for me; his altar
     A tender ram-lamb from our folds will often stain.
     He has allowed, as you can see, my cows to range
     And me to play what tune I please on the wild reed.
M. I am not envious, more amazed: the countryside's
     All in such turmoil. Sick myself, look, Tityrus,
     I drive goats forward; this one I can hardly lead.
     For here in the hazel thicket just now dropping twins,
     Ah, the flock's hope, on naked flint, she abandoned
         them.
     I keep remembering how the oak-trees touched of
         heaven,
     If we had been right-minded, foretold this evil time.
     But give us that god of yours: who is he, Tityrus?
T. The city men call Rome I reckoned, Melibóeus,
     Fool that I was, like this of ours, to which we
         shepherds

Are often wont to drive the weanlings of the ewes.
So puppies are like dogs, I knew, so kids are like
Their mother goats, so I'd compare big things to
    small.
But she has raised her head among the other cities
High as a cypress-tree above the guelder-rose.

M. And what was your great reason, then, for seeing
    Rome?

T. Liberty, which, though late, looked kindly on the
    indolent,
After my beard fell whiter to the barber's trim,
Looked kindly, though, and after a long while
    arrived,
After Amaryllis had us and Galatéa left.
For (yes, I will confess) while Galatea held me,
There was no hope of liberty nor thought of thrift.
Though many a sacrificial victim left my pens,
And much cream cheese was pressed for the
    ungrateful city,
My right hand never came back home heavy with
    bronze.

M. I wondered, Amaryllis, why you wept and called
To the gods – for whom you left fruit hanging on
    the tree;
Tityrus was away. The very pines, Tityrus,
The very springs, these very orchards called to you.

T. What could I do? For nowhere else could I escape
From slavery or meet divinities so present.
It was here I saw him, Meliboeus, the young man
For whom twice six days every year our altar smokes.

It was here to my petition he first gave reply:
'Graze cattle as before, my children, and yoke bulls.'

M. Lucky old man, the land then will remain your own,
And large enough for you, although bare rock
    and bog
With muddy rushes covers all the pasturage:
No unaccustomed feed will try your breeding ewes,
And no infection harm them from a neighbour's flock.
Lucky old man, among familiar rivers here
And sacred springs you'll angle for the cooling shade;
The hedge this side, along your neighbour's
    boundary,
Its willow flowers as ever feeding Hybla bees,
Will often whisper you persuasively to sleep;
The pruner under that high bluff will sing to the
    breeze,
Nor yet meanwhile will cooing pigeons, your own
    brood,
Nor turtledove be slow to moan from the airy elm.

T. Then sooner will light-footed stags feed in the sky
And ocean tides leave fishes naked on the shore,
Sooner in exile, wandering through each other's land,
Will Parthian drink the Arar, or Germany the Tigris,
Than from our memory will his face ever fade.

M. But *we* must leave here, some for thirsty Africa,
Others for Scythia and Oäxes' chalky flood
And the Britanni quite cut off from the whole world.
Look, shall I ever, seeing after a long while
My fathers' bounds and my poor cabin's turf-heaped
    roof,

3

Hereafter marvel at my kingdom – a few corn-ears?
Some godless veteran will own this fallow tilth,
These cornfields a barbarian. Look where strife
    has led
Rome's wretched citizens: we have sown fields for
    these!
Graft pear-trees, Meliboeus, now, set vines in rows.
Go, little she-goats, go, once happy flock of mine.
Not I hereafter, stretched full length in some green
    cave,
Shall watch you far off hanging on a thorny crag;
I'll sing no songs; not in my keeping, little goats,
You'll crop the flowering lucerne and bitter willow.

T. However, for tonight you could rest here with me
Upon green leafage: I can offer you ripe fruit
And mealy chestnuts and abundance of milk cheese.
Far off the roof-tops of the farms already smoke
And down from the high mountains taller
    shadows fall.

Eclogue II

For beautiful Alexis, the master's favourite,
Shepherd Córydon burned, and knew he had no hope.
Only, he used to walk each day among the dense
Shady-topped beeches. There, alone, in empty longing,
He hurled this artless monologue at hills and woods:
    'O cruel Alexis, have you no time for my tunes?
No pity for us? You'll be the death of me at last.
Now, even the cattle cast about for cool and shade,
Now even green lizards hide among the hawthorn brakes,
And Thestylis, for reapers faint from the fierce heat,
Is crushing pungent pot-herbs, garlic and wild thyme.
But I, while vineyards ring with the cicadas' scream,
Retrace your steps, alone, beneath the burning sun.
Had I not better bide the wrath of Amaryllis,
Her high-and-mighty moods? Better endure Menalcas,
However black he were and you however blond?
O lovely boy, don't trust complexion overmuch:
White privet flowers fall, black bilberries are picked.
You scorn me, Alexis, never asking who I am,
How rich in flocks, how affluent in snowy milk.
My thousand ewe-lambs range the hills of Sicily;
Come frost, come summer, never do I lack fresh milk.
I play the tunes Amphíon used, when he called cattle,
Dircéan Amphion on Actéan Aracýnthus.
I'm not that ugly: on the beach I saw myself
Lately, when sea stood wind-becalmed. With you as judge
I'd not be scared of Daphnis, if mirrors tell the truth.

5

O if you'd only fancy life with me in country
Squalor, in a humble hut, and shooting fallow deer,
And shepherding a flock of kids with green hibiscus!
Piping beside me in the woods you'll mimic Pan
(Pan pioneered the fixing fast of several reeds
With bees-wax; sheep are in Pan's care, head-shepherds
    too);
You'd not be sorry when the reed callused your lip:
What pains Amyntas took to master this same art!
I have a pipe composed of seven unequal stems
Of hemlock, which Damoetas gave me when he died,
A while ago, and said, "Now she owns you, the second,"
Damoetas said; Amyntas envied me, the fool.
Two chamois kids, besides, I found in a sheer coomb.
Their hides are dappled even now with white; they drain
One ewe's dugs each a day; I'm keeping them for you,
Though Thestylis has long desired to take them from me;
She'll do it too, since you regard our gifts as crude.
Come here, O lovely boy: for you the Nymphs bring lilies,
Look, in baskets full; for you the Naiad fair,
Plucking pale violets and poppy heads, combines
Narcissus with them, and the flower of fragrant dill;
Then, weaving marjoram in, and other pleasant herbs,
Colours soft bilberries with yellow marigold.
Myself, I'll pick the grey-white apples with tender down,
And chestnuts, which my Amaryllis used to love;
I'll add the waxy plum (this fruit too shall be honoured),
And I'll pluck you, O laurels, and you, neighbour myrtle,
For so arranged you mingle pleasant fragrances.
Corydon, you're a yokel; Alexis scorns your gifts,

Nor could you beat Iollas in a giving-match.
Alas, what have I done, poor lunatic, unleashing
Auster on flower-beds and wild boar on clear springs!
Ah, you are mad to leave me. Gods have dwelt in woods,
Dardanian Paris too. Pallas can keep her cities,
But let the woods beyond all else please you and me.
Grim lions pursue the wolf, wolves in their turn the goat,
Mischievous goats pursue the flowering lucerne,
And Corydon you, Alexis – each at pleasure's pull.
Look, oxen now bring home their yoke-suspended
      ploughs,
And the sun, going down, doubles growing shadows;
But I burn in love's fire: can one set bounds to love?
Ah, Corydon, Corydon, what madness mastered you!
You've left a vine half-pruned upon a leafy elm:
Why not at least prepare to weave of osiers
And supple rushes something practical you need?
If this Alexis sneers at you, you'll find another.'

Eclogue IV

Sicilian Muses, grant me a slightly grander song.
Not all delight in trees and lowly tamarisks;
Let woods, if woods we sing, be worthy of a consul.
    Now the last age of Cumae's prophecy has come;
The great succession of centuries is born afresh.
Now too returns the Virgin; Saturn's rule returns;
A new begetting now descends from heaven's height.
O chaste Lucina, look with blessing on the boy
Whose birth will end the iron race at last and raise
A golden through the world: now your Apollo rules.
And, Pollio, this glory enters time with you;
Your consulship begins the march of the great months;
With you to guide, if traces of our sin remain,
They, nullified, will free the lands from lasting fear.
He will receive the life divine, and see the gods
Mingling with heroes, and himself be seen of them,
And rule a world made peaceful by his father's virtues.
    But first, as little gifts for you, child, Earth untilled
Will pour the straying ivy rife, and baccaris,
And colocasia mixing with acanthus' smile.
She-goats unshepherded will bring home udders plumped
With milk, and cattle will not fear the lion's might.
Your very cradle will pour forth caressing flowers.
The snake will perish, and the treacherous poison-herb
Perish; Assyrian spikenard commonly will grow.
And then, so soon as you can read of heroes' praise

And of your father's deeds, and know what manhood
      means,
Soft spikes of grain will gradually gild the fields,
And reddening grapes will hang in clusters on wild brier,
And dewy honey sweat from tough Italian oaks.
Traces, though few, will linger yet of the old deceit,
Commanding men to tempt Thetis with ships, to encircle
Towns with walls, to inflict deep furrows on the Earth.
There'll be a second Tiphys then, a second Argo
To carry chosen heroes; there'll even be second wars,
And once more great Achilles will be sent to Troy.
Later, when strength of years has made a man of you,
The carrier too will quit the sea, no naval pines
Barter their goods, but every land bear everything.
The soil will suffer hoes no more, nor vines the hook.
The sturdy ploughman too will now unyoke his team,
And wool unlearn the lies of variable dye,
But in the fields the ram himself will change his fleece,
Now to sweet-blushing murex, now to saffron yellow,
And natural vermilion clothe the grazing lambs.
    'Speed on those centuries', said the Parcae to their
      spindles,
Concordant with the steadfast nod of Destiny.
O enter (for the time approaches) your great glory,
Dear scion of gods, great aftergrowth of Jupiter!
Look at the cosmos trembling in its massive round,
Lands and the expanse of ocean and the sky profound;
Look how they all are full of joy at the age to come!
O then for me may long life's latest part remain
And spirit great enough to celebrate your deeds!

Linus will not defeat me in song, nor Thracian Orpheûs,
Though one should have his father's aid and one his
      mother's,
Orpheus Callíopë and Linus fair Apollo.
If Pan too challenged me, with Arcady as judge,
Pan too, with Arcady as judge, would own defeat.

  Begin, small boy, to know your mother with a smile
(Ten lunar months have brought your mother long
      discomfort)
Begin, small boy: him who for parent have not smiled
No god invites to table nor goddess to bed.

Eclogue V

Me. Why don't we, Mopsus, meeting like this, good men
both,
    You to blow the light reeds, I to versify,
    Sit down together here where hazels mix with elms?

Mo. You're senior, Menalcas; I owe you deference,
    Whether we go where fitful Zephyrs make uncertain
    Shade, or into the cave instead. See how the cave
    Is dappled by a woodland vine's rare grape-clusters.

Me. Only Amyntas in our hills competes with you.

Mo. What? He might just as well compete to outplay
Phoebus.

Me. Then, Mopsus, you start first – with Phyllis' flames
perhaps
    Or Alcon's praises or a flyting against Codrus.
    You start, and Tityrus will watch the grazing kids.

Mo. No, I'll try out the song I wrote down recently
    On green beech bark, noting the tune between the
lines:
    Then you can tell Amyntas to compete with me.

Me. As surely as tough willow yields to the pale olive,
    Or humble red valerian to the crimson rose,
    So does Amyntas in our judgement yield to you.
    But no more talk, lad: we have come into the cave.

Mo. The Nymphs for Daphnis, cut off by a cruel death,

Shed tears (you streams and hazels witness for the
    Nymphs),
When, clasping her own son's poor body in her arms,
A mother called both gods and stars alike cruel.
In those days there were none who drove their
    pastured cattle
To the cool rivers, Daphnis; no four-footed beast
Would either lap the stream or touch a blade of grass.
The wild hills, Daphnis, and the forests even tell
How Punic lions roared in grief at your destruction.
Daphnis ordained to yoke Armenian tigresses
To chariots, Daphnis to lead on the Bacchic rout
And twine tough javelins with gentle foliage.
As vines are glorious for trees, as grapes for vines,
As bulls for herds, and standing crops for fertile
    fields,
You are all glory to your folk. But since fate took you,
Apollo's self and Pales' self have left the land.
From furrows we have often trusted with large barleys
Are born unlucky darnel and the barren oat.
For the soft violet, for radiant narcissus,
Thistles spring up and paliurus with sharpened
    spines.
Scatter the ground with petals, cast shade on the
    springs,
Shepherds, (that such be done for him is Daphnis'
    will),
And make a mound and add above the mound a song:
Daphnis am I in woodland, known hence far as the stars,
Herd of a handsome flock, myself the handsomer.

Me. For us your song, inspired poet, is like sleep
On meadow grass for the fatigued, or in the heat
Quenching one's thirst from a leaping stream of sweet
     water.
You equal both your master's piping and his voice.
Lucky lad! From now on you'll be second to him.
Yet we, no matter how, will in return recite
This thing of ours, and praise your Daphnis to the stars –
Yes, to the stars raise Daphnis, for Daphnis loved
     us too.

Mo. What greater service could you render us than that?
The lad himself deserved singing, and Stimichon
Some time ago spoke highly of your song to us.

Me. Daphnis in white admires Olympus' strange
     threshold,
And sees the planets and the clouds beneath his feet.
Therefore keen pleasure grips forest and countryside,
Pan also, and the shepherds, and the Dryad maids.
The wolf intends no ambush to the flock, the nets
No trickery to deer: Daphnis the good loves peace.
For gladness even the unshorn mountains fling their
     voices
Toward the stars; now even the orchards, even the
     rocks
Echo the song: 'A god, a god is he, Menalcas!'
O bless your folk and prosper them! Here are four
     altars:
Look, Daphnis, two for you and two high ones for
     Phoebus.
Two goblets each, frothing with fresh milk, every year

And two large bowls of olive oil I'll set for you;
And best of all, gladdening the feast with Bacchus'
    store
(In winter, by the hearth; at harvest, in the shade),
I'll pour Ariusian wine, fresh nectar, from big stoups.
Damoetas and the Lyctian Aegon will sing for me;
Alphesiboeus imitate the Satyrs' dance.
These offerings ever shall be yours, both when we pay
The Nymphs our solemn vows and when we purge the
    fields.
So long as fish love rivers, wild boar mountain
    heights,
So long as bees eat thyme, and the cicada dew,
Always your honour, name and praises will endure.
As farmers every year to Bacchus and to Ceres,
So they will vow to you; you too will claim their vows.

Mo. What can I give you, what return make for such song?
For neither does the whistling of Auster coming
Sound so pleasant to me, nor beaches beaten by
    waves,
Nor rivers rushing down the valleys among rocks.

Me. We shall present you first with this frail hemlock pipe.
This taught us 'Corydon burned for beautiful Alexis';
This also taught us 'Whose flock? Meliboeus his?'

Mo. You take the crook, then, which Antígenes failed
    to get
For all his asking (lovable as then he was),
A handsome thing, with matching knobs and brass,
                          Menalcas.

Eclogue VI

With Syracusan verses our Thaléa first
Thought fit to play, nor blushed to live among the woods.
When I was singing kings and battles, Cynthius pulled
My ear in admonition: 'A shepherd, Tityrus,
Should feed his flock fat, but recite a thin-spun song.'
I now (for you'll have many eager to recite
Your praises, Varus, and compose unhappy wars)
Will meditate the rustic Muse on slender reed.
I sing to order. Yet if any read this too,
If any love-beguiled, Varus, our tamarisks
Will sing of you, each grove of you, nor any page
Please Phoebus more than that headed by Varus' name.
    Proceed, Piéridës. Young Chromis and Mnasyllos
Once saw Silenus lying in a cave asleep,
His veins, as ever, swollen with yesterday's Iacchus;
Only, the garlands lay apart, fallen from his head,
And from its well-worn handle a heavy tankard hung.
Attacking (for the old man had often cheated both
With hope of song) they bind him with his own garlands.
Aeglë joins in, arriving as they grow alarmed,
Aeglë of Naiads loveliest, and, now he's looking,
With blood-red mulberries paints his temples and his brow.
The trick amuses him, but 'Why the bonds?' he asks;
'Release me, lads; it is enough to have shown your power.
Now hear the song you want; your payment shall be song,
Hers of another kind.' And with that he begins.
Then truly you could see Fauns and wild animals

Playing in rhythm, then stubborn oaks rocking their
    crowns.
Not so much joy does Phoebus bring Parnassus' crag,
Nor Orpheûs so astonish Rhódopë and Ísmarus.
    For he was singing how through a great emptiness
The seeds of earth and breath and sea and liquid fire
Were forced together; how from these first things all else,
All, and the cosmos' tender globe grew of itself;
Then land began to harden and in the deep shut off
Nereûs and gradually assume the shapes of things;
And now the dawn of the new sun amazes earth,
And showers fall from clouds moved higher overhead,
When first the forest trees begin to rise, and when
Rare creatures wander over unfamiliar hills.
Here he recounts the stones by Pyrrha thrown, Saturnian
Kingship, Caucasian eagles and Prometheus' theft;
Adds at what fountain mariners for Hylas lost
Shouted till all the shore re-echoed *Hylas, Hylas*;
And (fortunate if herds of kine had never been)
Consoles Pasíphaë for love of a white steer.
Unlucky maiden, ah, what madness mastered you!
The Proetides with mimic lowing filled the fields,
But yet not one pursued so base an intercourse
With beasts, although she feared the plough's yoke for her
    neck
And many a time would feel on her smooth brow for horns.
Unlucky maiden, ah, you wander now on mountains,
But he, with snow-white flank pressing soft hyacinth,
Beneath black ilex ruminates the sallow grass,

Or tracks some female in a great herd. 'Close, you Nymphs,
Dictéan Nymphs, now close the clearings in the woods.
Somewhere, perhaps, the wandering hoof-prints of a bull
Will find their own way to our eyes; possibly he,
Attracted by green grass, or following the herd,
Is led on by some cow to Gortyn's cattle-sheds.'
Then sings he the maid who admired Hesperidéan apples;
Then with the moss of bitter bark surrounds and lifts
The Phaëthóntiads from earth as alders tall;
Then sings of Gallus wandering by Permessus' stream,
How one of the Sisters led him to Aonia's mountains,
And how all Phoebus' choir stood up to greet a man;
How Linus there, the shepherd of inspired song,
His locks adorned with flowers and bitter celery,
Told him: 'The Muses give you this reed pipe (there,
    take it)
Which once they gave the old Ascréan, whose melody
Could draw the stubborn rowans down the mountainside.
Tell you with this the origin of Grynia's grove,
Lest any sacred wood be more Apollo's pride.'
    Why should I speak of Nisus' Scylla, who (so runs
The rumour), white groin girdled round with barking
    monsters,
Tossed the Dulichian ships and in her deep whirlpool
With sea-hounds, ah, would savage frightened mariners?
Or how he told the tale of Tereûs' limbs transformed,
What feast, what present Philomel prepared for him,
By what route sought the wilderness, and on what wings
Before that swooped unhappy over her own roof?

All, that from Phoebus' meditation, in old days, blest
Eurotas heard and bade his laurels memorize,
He sings (the smitten valleys tell it to the stars),
Till Vesper came to view in a reluctant sky
And bade the flock be folded and their number told.

Eclogue VII

MELIBOEUS

M. Daphnis was seated once beneath a rustling ilex,
And Corydon and Thyrsis had combined their flocks,
Corydon she-goats milk-distended, Thyrsis ewes,
Both in the flower of their ages, Arcadians both,
Well-paired at singing and prepared to cap a verse.
Here, while I shielded tender myrtles from the cold,
My herd's old man, the he-goat, had wandered off;
 and then
I notice Daphnis. 'Quick,' he says, at sight of me,
'Come here, Meliboeus, (your he-goat and the kids
 are safe)
And rest in shade, if you can take time off. The steers
Will find their own way through the meadows here to
 drink.
Here Mincius fringes his green banks with tender
 reeds,
And swarms of bees are humming from the
 sacred oak.'
So what was I to do? I had no Phyllis, no
Alcippë at home to pen the lambs I'd lately weaned,
And a great match was promised – Corydon v.
 Thyrsis;
However, I postponed my business for their play.
They therefore both began competing in alternate
Verses; the Muses wished alternatives recalled.

These Corydon delivered, Thyrsis those, in turn.

C.   Nymphs, our belov'd, Libethrians, either grant me
      song
  Such as you grant my Codrus (he is second best
  At verse to Phoebus), or, if we can't all succeed,
  Here on the sacred pine shall hang a tuneful pipe.

T. Shepherds, with ivy decorate the rising poet,
  Arcadians, so that Codrus burst his guts with envy;
  Or, if he praise beyond what pleases, bind my brow
  With baccar, lest an ill tongue harm the bard to be.

C.   For you this bristling boar's head, Delia, from little
  Mico, and the branching antlers of a long-lived stag.
  If this good luck be lasting, you shall stand
      full-length
  In smoothest marble, calves enlaced in scarlet boots.

T. A bowl of milk each year, Priapus, and these cakes
  Are all you need expect; you guard a poor man's
      patch.
  Our present means have made you marble; none the
      less,
  If lambing-time recruit the flock, you shall be gold.

C.   Nerínë Galatéa, sweeter than Hyblan thyme,
  Whiter to me than swans, more shapely than pale ivy,
  Soon as the bulls return from pasture to the byre,
  If you have any care for your Corydon, come to him.

T. Nay, you can think me sourer than Sardinia's herb,
  Rougher than broom, cheaper than seaweed tossed
      ashore,
  If this day's light's not longer than twelve months
      to me.

Go home from pasture, shame upon you, bull-
    calves, go.

C.   You mossy springs, and meadow-grass softer than
      sleep,

And that arbutus green whose rare shade covers you,
Fend off the solstice from the flock: now summer
    comes
Scorching; now buds are bursting on the tough
    vine-branch.

T. Here's hearth and pitch-pine billets, here's a roaring
    fire
Ever alight, and doorposts black with ingrained soot.
We mind the freezing cold of Boreas here no more
Than the wolf numbers, or torrential streams their
    banks.

C.   Still are the junipers, and the prickly Spanish
      chestnuts;
Beneath each tree her fruit is lying strewn around;
Now everything is laughing: but if fair Alexis
Should leave these hills, you'd even see the streams
    run dry.

T. Parched fields and thirsty grass, dying of tainted air;
Liber begrudges tendrilled shade to these hillsides:
But when our Phyllis comes, each coppice will be
    green,
And Jove descend abundantly in merry rain.

C.   Dearest the poplar to Alcídes, vines to Bacchus,
Myrtle to lovely Venus, to Phoebus his own bay.
Phyllis loves hazels, and, while those are Phyllis' love,
Hazels will never lose to myrtle, or Phoebus' bay.

T. Fairest the ash in forest, in pleasure-gardens pine,
  Poplars by streams, and on high mountains silver fir:
  But visit me more often, lovely Lycidas,
  And forest ash and garden pine will honour you.

M. This I remember, and how Thyrsis lost the match.
  For us, from that day, Corydon's been Corydon.

Eclogue IX

L. Where do feet lead you, Moeris? Like the road, to
    town?

M. Oh, Lycidas, we've lived to reach this – that a stranger
    (Something we never feared) should seize our little
        farm
    And say: 'This property is mine; old tenants, out!'
    Defeated now, sad that the world is Fortune's wheel,
    We take these kids (and may they bring bad luck)
        to him.

L. Surely I'd heard that everything, from where the hills
    Begin to drop down, sloping gently from the ridge,
    Right to the water and the old beeches' broken crowns –
    That all this your Menalcas salvaged with his songs?

M. You had, and so the rumour ran; but songs of ours
    Avail among the War-God's weapons, Lycidas,
    As much as Chaonian doves, they say, when the eagle
        comes.
    Had not a raven on the left from the hollow ilex
    Warned me at all costs to cut short these new disputes,
    Your Moeris here would now be dead – Menalcas too.

L. Alas, who'd dream of such a crime? Alas, Menalcas,
    Your solace and yourself so nearly snatched from us!
    Then, who would sing *The Nymphs*? And who 'scatter
        the ground

With flowering herbs' or 'cast green shadows on the
    springs'?
Or there's the song I lately overheard from you,
The day you made your way to our darling Amaryllis:
'Tityrus, till I come (the way's short), feed the goats,
And drive them fed to water, Tityrus, and take care
While driving not to cross the he-goat – that one
    butts.'

M. Yes, and the song (still incomplete) he made for
    Varus:
'Varus, your name, if only Mantua be spared
(Ah, Mantua, too near, alas, to poor Cremona!),
Shall be uplifted to the stars by singing swans.'

L. As you would wish your swarms to shun Cyrnéan
    yews,
And clover-feed to swell the udders of your cows,
Begin, if you've anything. The Pierians have made
Me too a poet; I too have my songs; the shepherds
Even call me bard, but I do not believe them.
As yet I cannot rival Varius or Cinna,
But gabble like a gander among articulate swans.

M. I mean to, Lycidas; I'm thinking it out now,
Jogging my memory, for it's a famous song.
'Come here, O Galatéa. What sport is there in water?
Here it is radiant springtime; here by the riverside
Earth pours forth the pied flowers; here the white
    poplar leans
Over a cave, and limber vines weave tents of shade.
Come here, and leave the crazy waves to beat the
    beach.'

L.   What of that song I heard you sing one cloudless night
     Alone? I know the tune, if I could find the words:
     'Daphnis, why watch the ancient risings of the Signs?
     See where the star of Dionéan Caesar passes,
     The star when cornfields should rejoice in crops and
          when
     Grape-clusters on the sunny slopes should colour up.
     Graft pear-trees, Daphnis. Grandchildren will pick
          your fruit.'

M.   The years take all, one's wits included. I remember
     Often in boyhood singing the long suns asleep.
     So many songs I've now forgotten; even his voice
     Is failing Moeris now: the wolves saw Moeris first.
     Menalcas, though, will sing them for you often enough.

L.   You try our love too long with these apologies.
     And now the level sea's all hushed for you, and look
     How all the airs of the wind's murmuring have
          dropped.
     Here too we're halfway on our journey, for Bianor's
     Monument can just be seen. Here, where the farmers
     Strip the thick-grown leaves, here, Moeris, let us sing.
     Set down the kids here. We shall reach town just the
          same.
     Or, if afraid lest night, before then, turn to rain,
     We're free to walk on singing (the road will seem less
          hard).
     I'll take this load of yours, so we can walk and sing.

M.   No more of that, lad, and let's do what's urgent now;
     Then, when himself has come, the better we'll sing
     songs.

Eclogue X

Permit me, Arethusa, this last desperate task.
For Gallus mine (but may Lycóris read it too)
A brief song must be told; who'd deny Gallus song?
So, when you slide along below Sicanian waves,
May bitter Doris never taint you with her brine.
Begin then: let us tell of Gallus' troubled love,
While snub-nosed she-goats nibble at the tender shoots.
Not to the deaf we sing; the forests answer all.

    What woodlands or what rides detained you, Naiad
      maids,
When Gallus pined away of an unworthy love?
For not the summits of Parnassus, for not Pindus'
Delayed your presence, nor Aonian Aganippë.
The laurels even, even the tamarisks wept for him
Lying beneath a lonely cliff; even Maenalus'
Pine-forests wept for him, and cold Lycaeus' rocks.
And the sheep stand around; they think no shame of us,
Nor be you shamed, inspired poet, by the flock:
Lovely Adonis too fed sheep beside a stream.
The shepherd also came, the heavy swineherds came,
Menalcas came, wet through from steeping winter mast.
All ask him 'Whence that love of yours?' Apollo came;
'Gallus, you're mad!' he cried. 'Lycoris your beloved
Pursues another man through snows and horrid camps.'
Silvanus also came, with rustic honour crowned,
Tossing tall lilies on his head and fennel flowers.
Pan came, Arcadia's god, whom we ourselves have seen

Ruddled with elderberry blood and cinnabar.
'When will it end?' he said. 'Love cares not for such things;
You'll never glut cruel Love with tears, nor grass with
    streams,
Nor worker-bees with clover, nor she-goats with leaves.'
But sadly he replied: 'Arcadians, will you sing, though,
Of these things to your hills? You are supreme in song,
Arcadians. O how softly then my bones would rest,
If only your reed pipe hereafter told my love!
And how I wish that I'd been one of you, and either
Guarded your flock or harvested the ripened grapes!
For surely, were I mad on Phyllis or Amyntas
Or anyone (what if Amyntas is dark-skinned?
Dark too are violets, and bilberries are dark),
They'd lie with me among willows, under a limber vine;
Phyllis would gather garlands for me, Amyntas sing.
Here, Lycoris, are cool fountains, here soft fields,
Here woodland, here with you I'd be Time's casualty.
But now, demented love detains me under arms
Of callous Mars, amid weapons and opposing foes.
You, far from fatherland, (could I but disbelieve it!)
Gaze – ah, callous – on Alpine snows and frozen Rhine,
Alone, without me. Ah, may the frosts not injure *you*!
Ah, may the rough ice never cut *your* tender feet!
I'll go and tune to the Sicilian shepherd's oat
The songs I put together in Chalcidic verse.
The choice is made – to suffer in the woods among
The wild beasts' dens, and carve my love into the bark
Of tender trees: as they grow, so my love will grow.
But meanwhile with the Nymphs I'll range on Maenala

Or hunt the savage boar. No frosts will hinder me
From drawing coverts on Parthenium with hounds.
Already I see myself explore the sounding rocks
And groves, already long to shoot Cydonian darts
From Parthian horn – as if this remedied our madness,
Or that god learnt from human hardship to grow mild!
Now, once again, we take no joy in Hamadryads,
Nor even in song – again wish even the woods away.
No alteration can our labours make in him,
Not if we drank of Hebrus in the middle frosts
Of watery winter and endured Sithonian snows,
Nor if, when dying bark shrivels on the lofty elm,
Beneath the Crab we herded Ethiopian sheep.
Love conquers all: we also must submit to Love.'
    To have sung of these things, goddesses, while he sat
      and wove
A frail of slim hibiscus, will suffice your poet.
Pierians, you will make them very great, for Gallus –
Gallus, whose love so grows upon me hour by hour
As the green alder pushes upward in new spring.
Let us arise: for singers heavy is the shade,
Heavy the shade of juniper; and shade harms fruit.
Go, little she-goats, Hesper comes, go home replete.

The Georgics: Book Four

Onward. The celestial gifts of honey from the sky
I will sound. Attend this part as well, O Maecenas.
The wondrous spectacle of a tiny world –
bold-hearted princes, a whole nation's customs
and passions and citizens and wars will I describe for you.
In miniature my labour, but no miniature glory, if adverse
divinities allow it, if Apollo hears my prayer.

First, a settled site for your bees must be sought,
where no winds may access (for winds prevent them
bringing home their food), nor sheep or tussling kids
romp upon the flowers, nor rambling heifer in the
  meadows
to shake off the dew and erode the plantlife.
Keep gaudy lizards with their scaly backs
from the rich cells, and the bee-eater and other birds,
and Procne, breast stained with bloody hands.
For these devastate completely, far and wide, snatching
in their mouths bees on the wing, sweet snacks for their
  rough nestlings.
But let pure springs and pools greening with moss
be near, and a trickling stream slipping through the grass,
and let a palm or spreading oleaster overshade the
  vestibule,
so that when new kings lead out the first swarms
in dear spring and the youth frolic free of the honeycomb,
a nearby bank may woo them to dodge the heat

and a wayside tree may charm with its leafy welcome.
In mid-water, whether it tranquil pools or flows along,
pile willows and enormous rocks across
that upon bridges aplenty they may rest and open
wings to the summer sun, if perforce the eastwind
has sprinkled upon the slowpokes, or dunked them
     headfirst into the deep.
Hereabout let flourish green cassia and far-fragrant
thyme and a garland of savory with its heady exhalations,
and let violet beds drink from the gurgling spring.
As for the hives: whether you have one stitched
from hollow bark or woven of limber wicker
let it have narrow entrances, for winter with its chill
congeals honey, and heat streams it away runny.
Either offence against the bees must be feared the same:
not for nothing do they striving smear with wax
fine cracks in their rooms, and with flower-paste fill up
seams, and store up glue collected for this very purpose,
stickier than birdlime or the pitch of Phrygian Ida.
Often, if rumour's true, in dug-out burrows
underground they snug their home, or deep within
     pumice-pores
are found, or in the cavity of a rotting tree.
Either way, do slick with smooth mud their crazed chambers,
cosying them up, and toss a few leaves on top.
Neither allow a yew too near the hive, nor fire
the redding crab at your hearth, nor trust a sunken bog
or where the stench of swamp is strong, or where hollow
the struck rocks ring and the voice's echo ricochets back.

*

When in rout the golden sun has driven winter
beneath the earth and unveiled with summer light the sky,
O then they wing the glades and forests,
harvest purple blooms and lightly sip
the river's surface. For this, cheered with an unfamiliar glee,
they nestle nests and larvae, for this they skilful mould
fresh wax and fashion sticky honey.
Thus when you look up at their legion just unloosed
from the hive, up to the starred sky floating through liquid
       summer air,
and wonder at their cloud dark on the trailing wind,
take note: for sweet waters and sheltering leaves
they always beeline. Here scatter my prescribed delicacies:
rubbed balm, and tendrils of lowly waxflower,
and thrill up a tinkling sound, shaking Mother Cybele's
       cymbals all around.
On their own they'll settle upon the scented places, on
       their own
they'll burrow themselves by instinct in inmost chambers.

But if for battle they've burst forth – for often
between two kings strife with great riot swoops:
at once the rancour of the throng, the hearts churning
for war you can sense from afar. For a martial reveille
of raucous brass rattles the laggards, and a buzz
is heard like the broken blast of bugles.
Then all hopped-up they muster themselves, flash wings,
whet stingers with jaws and cinch up muscles,
and round the king right up to his battle-post thronged
they swarm and with great ruckus call out the foe.

Thus when they find a rainless spring day and open field
they charge from their coverts: *Clash!* Noise through
highest air, massed and bunched into a great ball
then headlong they crash! Not thicker hail from vast heaven
nor acorns hail so from the shaken oak.
The princes themselves among the battle lines with striking
       wings:
great hearts thump inside their tiny breasts,
ever so steadfast not to surrender till severe the victor
drives this side or that to turn tail in flight.
These tremors of passion, these battles so dire
with a little dust tossed are quelled and come to rest.

But when from the front you have recalled both
       commanders,
he who looks shabbier, lest he be a waste and a burden,
consign to extinction: let the better reign singly in his
       court.
He will glow with spots shagged in gold.
For two kinds there are: the nobler, distinguished in mien
and bright in burnished scales, the other unkempt
in his sloth, inglorious, dragging his fat paunch.
Just as the mould of kings is twofold, so too the
       commoners' bodies.
Some look rough and slovenly, as when out of thick dust
comes a wayfarer, parched, and spits dirt from his thirsty
mouth. Others gleam and fulgent flash
blazing in bodies trimmed with uniform flecks of gold:
this is the better breed, from these at the sky's appointed
       season

you will strain sweeter honey – so sweet, but more clear,
and fit to mellow the harsh taste of wine.

But when aimless flits the swarm, and gads about the sky,
and scorns the honeycombs, and leaves the hive to chill
you must curb their fickle spirits from these pointless
      antics.
It's no great task to curb them: you rip the kings' wings off –
while they cool their heels, no one will dare
take to the air or snatch up the banner from the encampment.
Let gardens breathing saffron flowers beckon,
and let the watchman against thieves and birds, guardian
Priapus of the Hellespont, protect with his willow-hook.
Let him whose care they are himself fetch thyme and pines
from mountain peaks, and plant them round about their
      lodge,
himself callous his hand with rugged work, himself plant
fruitful slips in the soil and water them with kind
      sprinklings.

Indeed, were I not fast upon the very end of my labours
furling sails, and rushing to nose my prow shoreward,
perhaps how care in tillage bedizens the lush garden
I'd sing, and the rosebeds of twice-blooming Paestum,
how the chicory exults in the brook it drinks,
and the banks green in celery, and how twining through its
      vines
the cucumber swells into corpulence; nor should I keep
      silent
on late-blooming narcissus or the stalk of supple acanthus,
pale ivies and shore-loving myrtles.

For I remember how, beneath the towers of Tarentum's
    citadel
where dark Galaesus waters the golden fields,
I saw an old Corycian, who had a few acres
of godforsaken land – a patch not fertile for the plough-ox
nor fit for flocks nor favourable for the vine.
Yet here, planting well-spaced vegetables among the scrub,
white lilies and verbena, and the flimsy poppy,
in cheer he matched the wealth of kings, and late returning
home at night he loaded his table with banquets unbought.
First in spring to pluck roses, first in fall to pick apples,
and when lowering winter was still cracking rocks
with cold, and with ice bridling the coursing stream,
he was already cutting back the soft hyacinth's old growth,
chiding tardy summer and the westwind's delay.
Therefore this man was first to luxuriate in brood-bees
and an abundant swarm, first to collect foamy honey
from the squeezed comb, his lindens and pines most lush
and as many buds as his lavish tree bedecks itself
in early bloom, so many fruits it holds in ripe autumn.
What's more, mature the elms he set in widespread rows,
hard-barked the pear trees, blackthorns already bearing sloes,
the plane tree already providing shade for carouses.
But I prevented by my too-slight space
pass silent on and leave that tale for others after me.

Now come: I will unfold what nature
Jupiter himself bestowed on bees, for which reward
following the ringing chants and clashing bronzes of the
    Curetes

they had fed the king of heaven deep within a Dictaean
    cave.
They alone in common rear their young, in partnership
    they hold
their city's habitations, and live out their lives under
    sovereign laws,
they alone recognize a fatherland and constant home,
and mindful of the coming winter endure summer toil
and in common store lay in their gleanings.
For some have charge of provisions, and by settled compact
busy in the fields; some within their houses' walls
lay down tears of the narcissus and sticky sap
from tree-bark as the first foundation of the hive, then
    drape up
viscous wax. Others train out the nation's hope,
the full-grown hatch; others pack in purest
honey, swelling the cells with liquid nectar.
There are those to whom guard duty at the gates falls
    by lot;
in turn they eye heaven's showers and overcast,
or receive loads from incomers, or in mustered squads
blockade the drones (that shiftless ruck) from the stalls.
The industry glows, and the fragrant honey breathes of
    thyme.
As when the Cyclopes from malleable ore
work lightning bolts, some with ox-hide bellows
suck and blow the air, others dunk the screaming bronze
in a cistern; Aetna groans beneath its anvilled charge;
they heave their arms with mighty force in alternating
rhythm, and turn the metal with pincing tongs:

just so, if one may small compare with great,
an innate love of gain pricks on Athenian bees
each in his own capacity. The elders warden the towns,
fortify the hives and fashion daedal chambers.
Worn out, the young ones drag themselves home far into
    night,
legs thick with thyme. They feast on arbutes all around,
on grey-green willows, on cassia and red-flecked crocus,
on the sappy linden and dusky hyacinths.
Together their rest from labour, together their labour:
at dawn they rush out their gates, no dilly-dally; and when
    at last
the evening star exhorts them quit their forage
afield, then they head for their hutches, then restore their
    bodies.
A buzzing: they murmur around the doors and on the
    doorsteps.
Later, when they've tucked themselves into their chambers,
    hushed
is the night, well-earned sleep overtakes their tuckered limbs.
But truly, rain threatening, they don't venture far from
    their stalls
nor trust the sky when the eastwind advances,
but on all sides, safe beneath the city's ramparts, siphon up
    water
and attempt short sorties, and often take up pebbles, with
    which,
as a skiff unsteady on the tossing wave takes on ballast,
they balance themselves through the flimsy cloud.

*

You will marvel *this* custom has found favour among bees:
they indulge not in lovemaking, nor slacken their sinews
sluggish in venery, nor birth young in travail,
but alone the females gather up their children in their mouths
from leaves and herbs delectable, unmated they provide a
    king
and tiny citizens, and remodel their courts and waxy realms.
Often too, wandering among jagged flint they scrape
their wings, and freely give their lives under their load:
so great their love of flowers and the glory of
    honey-making.
Thus although the limit of a slender age awaits each one
(for never more than seven summers it's unskeined)
yet the race endures immortal, through unnumbered years
    stands fast
the fortune of the house, and their pedigree records
    ancestors of ancestors.

What's more, not Egypt nor great Lydia, nor the Parthian
    peoples,
nor the Hydaspean Medes so venerate their king.
Their king unharmed, the swarm has a single mind;
if lost, they break faith, tear down their stockpiled honey
and themselves dismantle the trellises of the hive.
He is protector of their works, him they revere and all
surround him with crowded noise and pack him in
    thronging,
and often lift him to their shoulders, and throw their bodies
into battle seeking among the wounds a beautiful death.

*

Following such signs and such habits, some
have said that bees enjoy a share of the divine mind
and ethereal draughts. For God moves through all things –
lands and the sea's expanse and deepest heaven.
Flocks, herds, men, all breeds of beasts . . .
from Him each at birth draws its fine-spun life,
it seems, and to Him all return at last: all things undone
restored, no place for death, but alive they fly
into the station of a star and mount to heaven's zenith.

If ever you want to breach the bees' tight courts, and uncache
hoarded honey from their treasuries, first with a handful of
    water
spritz and freshen your mouth, and hold out penetrating
    smoke.
Their rage surpasses measure: hurt, they breathe venom
into their stings, leave their stingers unseen
stuck in the vein, and lay down their lives in the wound.
Twice men gather the lavish yield, two seasons the harvest:
soon as Pleiad Taygete has shown her heavenly face
to earth and with her foot scorns the spurned flood of Ocean,
and when that same star fleeing rainy Pisces
more sadly sinks down from the sky into the wintry waves.
But if you fear a harsh winter, and would spare their future
and pity their crushed spirits and shattered fortunes, –
yet who to fumigate with thyme and prune off disused cells
would hesitate? For often unnoticed the newt has nibbled
the honeycombs, or whole dens of light-fleeing
    cockroaches,
or the no-account drone bellies up to another's ration,

or the vicious hornet has engaged their unequal arms
or the malevolent race of moths, or the spider spited by
    Minerva
has hung in the aisles her loose webs.
The more they're plundered, the more doggedly they'll
    press
to repair the wrack of their fallen race:
they'll cram the galleries and weave their garners about
    with nectar.

But if (since life has brought to bees our calamities too)
their bodies droop under grim disease –
which instantly you can discern by no vague signs:
sick, their colour changes at once, ragged leanness
disfigures their looks, then the bodies of those deprived of
    life
they bear out from their homes and lead the funeral march,
or linked by their feet they hang from the doorways,
or shut within chambers they linger, all
listless with starvation and numb with pinching cold.
Then a sound is heard, lower, a drawn-out mutter,
as sometimes cold the southwind hushes through the trees,
as the sea hisses roiling in its outflowing swell,
as seethes in shut furnaces the furious blaze.
Now I suggest you burn fragrant galbanum
and run in honey through straws of reed
heartening them, calling the weary to familiar food.
It will help, too, to mix the flavour of pounded gall-nuts
with dried roses, or must made concentrate
over a good fire, or raisin-wine from the Psithian vine,

and Athenian thyme with heady-smelling centaury.
There also is a flower in the meadows, to which the name
     amellus
farmers gave, an easy plant to ferret out,
for from one clump it lifts a massy spray –
itself golden, but in its petals which splay thickly around
crimson sheens beneath dark violet;
often the gods' altars are garlanded with its woven wreaths,
bitter on the tongue its taste, in grazed vales
shepherds gather it, and near the winding waters of Mella.
Boil its roots in fragrant wine
and set it at their doors for food in heaping baskets.

But if a man's whole hive suddenly has failed
and he knows not whence to revive the breed in a new line,
time to unfold the famed discovery of the Arcadian master
and by what means the spoiled blood from slain bullocks
has often engendered bees. I'll unspool
the whole account, retracing from its earliest source.
For where the blessed race of Pellaean Canopus
dwell near the Nile pooling in its sprawling stream
and ride their acres in painted skiffs,
where quivered Persia's territory hedges, and the river
onrushing, spilled unbroken down from the swart Indians,
branches into seven separate mouths
and with its black silt fertilizes Egypt green,
the whole region rests its sure well-being on this art.
First a spot – narrow and secluded for this very purpose –
is chosen: this with a narrow tile roof
and cramped walls they enclose, and add four windows

with slant light to front the four winds.
Then a calf with horns just arched upon his two-year brow
is fetched, with both his nostrils and the breath of his
     mouth,
despite great struggling, stopped up. After he's beaten to
     death
his carcass is pulped up, pounded through the unbroken
     hide.
They leave him lying thus in his pen, and stuff beneath his
     flanks
broken twigs, thyme and fresh cassia.
This is accomplished when first the Zephyrs drive the
     waves,
before the meadows blush so in new colour, before
chattering the swallow hangs her nest among the rafters.
Meanwhile, fluid warmed in the softening bones
stews, and creatures with ways wondrous to behold,
devoid of foot at first but soon buzzing at the wing,
brew up, and more and more take to the narrow air
until, like a shower poured from summer clouds
they burst forth, or like arrows from the plucked string
when light-armed Parthians engage the opening volley.

What god, O Muses, forged for us this art?
Whence did man's strange practice take its start?
The shepherd Aristaeus, flying Tempe on the Peneus
when his bees were lost (the story goes) to sickness and
     starvation,
lamenting stopped by the sacred spring at the stream's
     headwaters

much complaining, and prayed aloud his mother thus:
'Mother, O mother Cyrene, who commands these waters'
    depths,
why me? – why from the glorious line of gods
(if truly, as you claim, my father is Thymbraean Apollo)
did you bear me, hated by the Fates? Or where is your love
    of me
banished? Why did you enjoin me hope for heaven?
Look: even this very trophy of mortal life
which the skilful care of crops and herds had hardly
    hammered out
for me, for all my efforts, though you're my mother, I
    resign.
Nay – go and with your own hand uproot my fruitful
    orchards,
put hostile fire to my stables, destroy my harvest,
burn my crops and heft the stout axe against my vines,
if such spite for my glory has seized you!'

But his mother in her bedchamber beneath the river's
    depths
felt his clamour. Around her, nymphs spun Milesian fleeces
dyed with the deep colour of glass –
Drymo and Xantho and Ligea and Phyllodoce,
their hair poured shimmering upon their radiant necks,
Cydippe and golden Lycorias, one a maid,
the other having just suffered her first birth-pangs,
Clio and Beroe her sister, Ocean's daughters both,
both in gold, both in rainbowed hides arrayed,
and Ephyre and Opis and Asian Deiopea,

and last swift Arethusa with her arrows laid aside.
Among these Clymene gossiped of the frustrate vigilance
of Vulcan, of Mars' wiles and stolen pleasures,
and from Chaos on recounted the myriad loves of the gods.
While by this ballad captivated from the spindle they
     twisted
their soft work, again the grief of Aristaeus struck
his mother's ears, and upon their glassy chairs all
startled. But before the other sisters Arethusa
far surveying raised her golden head above the surface
     stream
and from afar: 'Your fright at so loud howling's not amiss,
O sister Cyrene! Himself, your dearest care,
Aristaeus heartsick by the waters of Father Peneus
stands weeping, and you he calls by name of *Cruelty*.'
To whom his mother, struck to the quick with sudden
     dread, cries:
'Go! Lead him! Lead him to us! He may tread this porch
     divine.'
And so she commanded the deep river to yawn
apart, that the youth might enter on foot. Hunched up
into mountain-shape the waters stood around him,
and welcomed him into a vast chasm, inviting him beneath
     the current.
Now wondering at his mother's home, a watery realm,
at lakes closed in caves and echoing groves,
he went on, astonished by the mighty rush of waters –
every river gliding beneath the wide earth
he descried, distinct in their courses: Phasis and Lycus,
the spring from which deep Enipeus first jets forth,

from which Father Tiber, from which the Anian stream
and rocky raucous Hypanis, and Mysian Caicus,
and Eridanus, both horns on his bullish front gilt,
than which no other stream more violent flows
out over fertile farmland into the purple sea.
When he's come into her chamber, its ceiling hung with
     pumice,
and Cyrene understands her son's vain tears,
her sisters timely minister to his hands
with clear spring water, and bring close-shorn napkins.
Some lade the table with a banquet and set down brimming
cups. The altars burn with Panchaian flame.
His mother declared: 'Lift your goblets of Maeonian wine:
we offer to Ocean.' With that she prayed
to Ocean, father of all, and the sister nymphs
who a hundred woods, a hundred rivers guard.
Thrice with liquid nectar she sprinkled the blazing hearth,
thrice the flame flared up anew, shooting to the rooftop.
With this omen bolstering his spirits, she thus began:

'There is in Neptune's Carpathian depths a seer,
aquamarine Proteus, who paces out the wide ocean
on a chariot yoked with fish and hippocampi.
Just now the ports of Thessaly and his native Pallene
he revisits; him the nymphs venerate and ancient
Nereus himself, for the seer has seen all –
what is, what has been, what's spun out soon to come,
for such seemed good to Neptune, whose herds immense
of squalid seals he pastures beneath the swell.
Him, son, you first must clap in shackles, so that the whole

cause of malaise he may unriddle and rally your fortunes.
Without duress no counsel will he give, nor will you bend
      him
by imploring; turn stern force and chains upon your
        captive:
only against these his wiles will crash themselves to froth.
I myself, when the sun stokes up its midday heat,
when plants thirst and shade is more delightful to the flock,
will guide you to the old man's retreat, where weary from
        the waves
he withdraws, that you may come at him sprawled in easy
        sleep.
But when you hold him fast gripped in hands and shackles
then his multiform shapes will bamboozle you, and his
        wild-beast looks.
For suddenly he'll be a bristled boar, a deadly tigress,
a scaly dragon, a tawny-necked lioness,
or blast out the piercing hiss of flame and thus slip out
from his bonds, or melt into mere water and spill away.
But the more he turns himself into all shapes
the more, O son, hold firm his chains
until after his body's changing he is such
as you saw him when he lidded his eyes at the start of
        sleep.'

She spoke, and radiated ambrosia's pure perfume,
in which her son's whole body she enwrapped;
from his sleeked locks a sweet scent breathed,
and vigour came upon his nimble limbs. There is a spacious
        cavern

worn in a mountain's side, where by the wind many a wave
is driven and splits itself into secluded lagoons,
at times a safest anchorage for swamped mariners.
Inside, Proteus screens himself in the covert of a massive
    boulder.
Here the nymph stations the youth in ambush
away from the light; she herself waits far off, veiled in mist.
Soon the ravaging Dog Star which scorches the thirsty
    Indians
blazed in the firmament, and the fiery sun had devoured
    half
his wheel: the grasses parched, and sunken streams
baked in their dry throats, boiled down to slime by its rays,
when Proteus, seeking his usual cove came down
from the waves. Around him the race of the vast sea
revelled, sprayed briny droplets far and wide.
The seals stretched themselves out for sleep scattered along
    the shore.
He himself – just as at times the caretaker of cotes upon
    a hill
when the evening star leads home the calves from pasture
and with their bleating din the lambs whet the wolves –
sat on a rock in their midst and counted their number.
Now that Aristaeus gets his chance,
scarce he lets the old man settle his tired limbs
when with a mighty yell he rushes him, and claps him in
    shackles
where he lies. Proteus for his part not forgetful of his art
transforms himself into all wondrous things of the earth:
a flame, a horrible beast, a stream flowing.

But when no design wins deliverance, defeated
he returns to himself, and speaking at last with the mouth
     of a man
he asked, 'Now, sauciest youth, who charged you
to invade our home? What seek you here?' But Aristaeus:
'*You* know, Proteus – you above all know, nor can anything
     deceive you,
so *you* give up deceiving! Following the gods' behest
we come here, seeking an oracle for my flagging fortunes.'
So he intoned. At this the seer finally under sturdy force
rolled his eyes blazing with grey-green light
and savagely gnashing teeth thus unsealed his mouth with
     the fates:

'The wrath of no mean deity hounds you.
You do penance for a sore offence. Heartbroken Orpheus
     stirs up
these punishments against you (did not Fate intervene) –
far less than your deserving! – and rages tormented for his
     wife reft away.
Just so: headlong along the river that she might escape you,
doomed girl, she didn't see the monstrous snake
before her feet hugging the banks in tall grass.
The chorus of her companion dryads with wailing rimmed
the mountain's peaks, the crags of Rhodope mourned,
and alpen Pangaea, the martial land of Rhesus and the
     Getae,
the Hebrus mourned, and Orithyia the northwind's Attic
     bride.
But *he*, consoling love's agony with his hollow-shell lyre,

sang you, sweet wife, you to himself on the lonely shore,
you with the rising day, you at the day's decline.
Even the jaws of Taenarus, the steep gates of Dis,
the grove shrouded in black dread
he entered, and approached the dead, and their terrible
     king,
and the hearts unversed in gentling to human prayers.
But by his monody shaken from the deepest pits of Erebus
came wispy shades, and ghosts of those deprived of light,
as many as the birds that by the thousand hide themselves
     in leaves
when evening's star or winter sleet drives them from the
     mountains . . .
mothers and men and, emptied of life, the bodies
of bold-hearted heroes, boys and unwed maidens
and youths lain on the pyres before their parents' stares.
Around them the black mire and grotesque cattails
of Cocytus, revolting swamp that binds them with sluggish
     water
and Styx winding nine times around imprisons them.
Why, the very halls were astonished, and Death's inmost
Tartarus, and the Furies with livid snakes braided
in their hair, and Cerberus held agape his three mouths,
and the spin of Ixion's wheel halted with the wind.
And soon his steps retracing he had dodged every pitfall
and Eurydice restored was coming to the upper air
following behind (for that stipulation had Proserpina
     made)
when a sudden madness seized him, reckless loving –
truly forgivable, if Hell knew to forgive:

he stopped, and upon his own Eurydice, already at the very
    edge of light,
forgetful, alas! and his judgement overthrown . . . he
    looked back. Instantly
all his labour fell apart, broken the pitiless tyrant's pact,
and thrice thunder sounded over the pools of Avernus.
She cried, "O Orpheus, what has ruined wretched me
    and you,
what utter madness? Behold – again the cruel Fates
call me back, and darkness shrouds my swimming eyes!
And now, farewell – I am carried off cloaked in endless
    night,
stretching toward you helpless hands, O! yours no more!"
She cried, and sudden from his sight, like smoke mingling
into thin air, vanished away, and – as he clutched vainly
at shadows, longing to say so much . . . she never
saw him more, nor did the ferryman of Orcus
let him cross that swampy obstacle again.
What could he do? Where take himself, his wife twice
    snatched away?
With what sobs could he move Hades, with what word its
    powers?
Even now she was floating cold as death in the Stygian raft.
For seven whole months, month on month, they say,
beneath a skyscraping cliff by desolate Strymon's wave
he wept, and under the frozen stars spun out this song,
soothing tigers and enticing oaks with his dirge,
as mourning beneath the poplar shade the nightingale
laments her lost brood, which a rude ploughman
spying ripped unfledged from their nest, she sobs

49

nightlong, and on a branch perched her doleful song
renews, and fills full the sphere with dreary plaints.
No love, nor any wedding-song could bend his soul.
Lonely he would wander the Hyperborean ice, the
      snow-crusted Tanais,
the steppes ever widowed by Rhipaean frosts,
wailing Eurydice wrested away and the gift of Dis
annulled – by which devotion spurned, the Thracian
      dames
amid their consecrated rites and midnight bacchant orgies
tore the youth apart and scattered him across the field's
      expanse.
Even then, while down the middle of its rapids
the Hebrus, river of his father's realm, swept and rolled
his head ripped from its marble neck,
Eurydice his mere voice and cold tongue were calling,
O poor Eurydice as his spirit fled,
Eurydice the banks replied the whole river long.'

So said Proteus, and threw himself into the deep sea,
and where he dived the water whirled to foam beneath his
      vortex.
But Cyrene stayed. Unsought she addressed him, shaken:
'Son, you may lay down your soul's heavy care.
Here the whole cause of sickness, for this the nymphs
with whose troupe she used to trip through ancient groves
woeful brought this woeful blight upon your bees.
      Suppliant, you must extend
an offering, praying peace, and do homage to the lenient
      wood nymphs,

for they will grant pardon for your orisons, and ease their
    anger.
But first I will explain how you should supplicate in
    sequence:
select four choice bulls, outstanding in form,
who now with your herd graze the green ridge of Lycaeus,
and as many heifers with necks unworked.
For these erect four altars at the goddesses' high shrines,
and from their throats cascade the hallowed blood,
and leave their oxen carcasses in a leafy grove.
Later, when the ninth dawn flaunts her rising,
you will send Lethean poppies to Orpheus as a funeral
    offering
and sacrifice a black ewe, and return to the grove.
There honour Eurydice, now appeased, with a slaughtered
    calf.'
No delay – like a shot he performs his mother's
    instructions:
to the shrines he comes, rears the altars assigned,
leads in four choice bulls, outstanding in form
and as many heifers with necks unworked.
Later, when the ninth dawn had paraded her rising,
he sends a funeral offering to Orpheus and returns to the
    grove.
Here – . . . They spot a wonder, sudden and marvellous
to tell: in the oxens' liquified guts and through the whole
belly, bees buzz and swarm through the split flanks
and trail in unending clouds, and now surge
to a treetop and dangle in clusters from the limber boughs.

*

51

This I sang, about the care of fields and flocks
and about trees, while Caesar the great thundered in war
beside the deep Euphrates, and conqueror dealt out
laws to ready nations and pursued his course to heaven.
I, Virgil, at that time by sweet Parthenope
nurtured, flourishing in the study of inglorious leisure,
I who toyed with shepherd songs, and bold with youth,
sang you, Tityrus, beneath a vault of spreading beech.